Maps for the Modern World

Valerie June Hockett

Andrews McMeel
PUBLISHING®

Maps for the Modern World copyright © 2021 by Valerie June Hockett.
All rights reserved. Printed in China. No part of this book may be used
or reproduced in any manner whatsoever without written permission
except in the case of reprints in the context of reviews.

Andrews McMeel Publishing
a division of Andrews McMeel Universal
1130 Walnut Street, Kansas City, Missouri 64106

www.andrewsmcmeel.com

21 22 23 24 25 TEN 10 9 8 7 6 5 4 3 2 1

ISBN: 978-1-5248-5511-6

Library of Congress Control Number: 2020941222

Illustrations by Valerie June Hockett

Editor: Allison Adler
Art Director: Holly Swayne
Production Editor: Elizabeth A. Garcia
Production Manager: Carol Coe

ATTENTION: SCHOOLS AND BUSINESSES
Andrews McMeel books are available at quantity discounts with
bulk purchase for educational, business, or sales promotional use.
For information, please e-mail the Andrews McMeel Publishing
Special Sales Department: specialsales@amuniversal.com.

Enjoy *Maps for the Modern World* as an audiobook narrated by the
author, wherever audiobooks are sold.

In loving memory of Mary A. Burns

Foreword

When we reflect on the visible world, the reality of
suffering surrounds us every day. Whether our personal
suffering or the suffering of others, somewhere at
every moment there lives a tragedy. There lives poverty,
sickness, heartbreak, racism, hatred, injustice, and loss.
Maybe it's hope that keeps us carrying on, but where do
we find ourselves if we sit with the suffering? What does
it look like to create a more harmonious existence for all
beings with each breath?

The most transformative events of my life have occurred
when I found myself brave enough to face and truly examine
my fears. It's hard to fix a problem you don't realize
you have, so when a fear is revealed to me, I dare myself
to feel it fully. I challenge myself to mentally walk up
to it, let it roar in my face, knock me down, shatter my
heart, drown me trembling in sea-soaked tears, and rip
through me like a tornado, leaving no tree trunk rooted
and no tower untouched. It is only after I do that I
awaken to the reality that though the world may have
broken my heart, there is a stillness within that has not
been moved.

This book is a laboratory of poetic experiments in the
alchemy of life. While we all hope for a brighter world,
it can be difficult to see how to navigate through the
raging storms. I have to believe we are the creators of
the world we see each day and that the stillness that can
be felt in the wake of every storm holds the key to the
map of all change. A map that can be drawn only by your
own hand. How do we change the world? We change ourselves.

May the following poems inspire you to explore the
hemispheres and stratospheres, longitudes and latitudes,
boulevards, paths, roads, and avenues that lie within,
endlessly and patiently waiting to unfold.

Consciousness
& Awareness

It is a gift to be in a body—to inhabit a physical form—
and to be aware of the interconnectedness of all things.
Just as a device like our phone or computer allows us
to access the internet, our bodies enable us to access
universal consciousness. By centering ourselves in the
present moment—here and now—we can awaken infinite
beauty. Each moment holds an illuminated light that can
transform our reality. What do you wish to see?

Consciousness is connecting to the endless stream where
all things exist. It is like a portal to afternoon tea
with the mind of God where you want to hang around until
you are invited to stay for dinner. It is a library, a
seed bank, for all of creation here with you as you read
these words. It is impossible to separate yourself from
it, but it is sometimes so easy to forget that we have a
passport to the inner soul of the world.

Because all things exist in the realm of pure
consciousness, you can take your pick of which seeds you
want to water. Imagine you are the director of a film, and
it's time to capture the next scene. You say, *"Action!"* and
everyone starts to act out their part. Though the script
is written, every choice the players make can alter the

work. Life is the activation of the potential moments that already exist. Every element is already there, but before being activated, the moment is just a possibility. It is a still-life painting hanging on the wall of God's living room. Which possibilities will you activate for your life? What seeds will you gather from the conscious universe? What kind of world would you like to help create? What fruits and flowers would you like to grow in the garden of your life? What elements would you like to use for the play you are helping to write?

Since all things exist on the plane of universal consciousness, you can go ahead and claim your wishes and hopes as already done, but just because a seed is in the ground does not mean it will flower. You bring the seeds from the realm of consciousness back to the physical world where you will need to tend to them by the laws of physics — simple, right? Water and sun!

This is the only place.
It is your perspective
That must change
All planes exist here
All planes exist now
Same as in sadness
As in joy exist now
Same as it is day here
It is night somewhere, somehow.

So if you're looking for change
If you're searching for a place beyond
There must come a realization of
You, You as the one.

Meant for the grandest great,
The sweetest sweet,
The here and now,
The right on time,
The never late—

If you're looking for a place beyond
You must realize that
You, You are the sun
And your greatest work is yet to come!

—You Are the Sun

We are

I am

Here

To remind you

Of how

B-E-A-U-T-I-F-U-L

You are.

—Simple Sweet

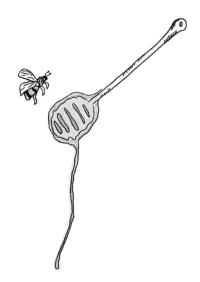

Skip

Skip

Watch

Skip

Bask

Bask Bask

Skip Skip

Watch Bask

Skip Watch

—Awareness

It is to live in the midst of great fortune.

It is to give more than expected.

It is to keep investing in a spirit bank

To know you have done all you could

And to trust that you will be guided

To the right place and always in the right time.

And how small you were—

How small we are—

We are small

In it all.

Small in it all.

Small in it all.

Small in it all.

Small in it all.

Small in it all.

Small in it all.

Small in it all.

Small in it all.

—Starlit Spaces

I want to be the voice that says:

"Be open to something beautiful!"

—Reincarnation / Do I Have to Have a Body?

The words were always written there
The book was on the shelf
The dust had gathered year by year
Beyond it lay a wealth.

Our nature had us touching screens
The pages never felt
A crisp, thin-weighted edge to turn
Was something we'd long left

The words—they fell upon the page
Before we first met time
They begged us to remember them
We promised, then raced on

We ran and ran but never reached
Our bodies heard the call
The book was opened
All was read
Of stories
Great and small
Reviewed was every moment spent
Each answer, question, all

The words were always written there
Their order was not clear
If we had chosen cautiously
They told a tale so dear
Of strength
Of courage
Bravery
In lands still ruled by fear

If we had chosen carefully
The words would sing like songs
Of wisdom, truth, and radiance
Of loss, but still made strong
A life of lives lived
One by one
Collected, bound, and shelved
Then multiplied by time
Each life a chapter

Turn the page
It's just begun
Between the lines and lives
We saw
Our word had been our wand
If we had wielded consciously
Life's treasure had been won.

—The Words

You will wonder why you ever cried
Why you ever felt the pain
When you realize nothing here can die
Only growing, ever change
And the mind can't comprehend this thought
Step beyond it
Truth will reign
Then you'll laugh
At how most things rational
From this angle are so strange

—Right Angle

When you're following your inner light,

You're always right.

—Right Light

If other planes exist
Why don't we see them here?

Because you must remember
And realize them
Here (place your hand over your heart)
First
Before they will appear.

Why does light exist?
Why is it important to shine?

All light shines in the direction of your realization.

Why is your current state not a hindrance
For your light
As long as the intention is there?

All light shines in the direction of your realization.

—The Hint

Kindness sprang off the page

And slapped me in the face

And I

Being me

Lost my shit completely

And whooped its ass—

Up and down the street

I, being me.

Ooooops.

I guess I fucked up.

—Recognize

There really are no guarantees
Please.
Only do the best you can
The rest will be the way it will be.

You really have no control
Pure soul.
There is a place between your eyes
Where light
And love
Shine
And bind along with life and time
And bless blissfully the undefined—
The beyond mind—
The stapled-fabled heart so blind.

You really have no other choice.
There really is no other way.
The stapled-fabled heart so blind
Must always choose to be sweet
To be kind.

—The Stapled-Fabled Heart

It is a planetary exploration
It is a self-examination
It is a constant, steady pacing
It is acknowledging what we are facing

And when you're settled in the moment
There,
There inside,
There comes a knowing
Of why you came and where you're going

And you can shape it how you want it
It was always a-waiting and a-wanting
To be molded, modeled, sculpted

There for all to have and hold it.

—Consciousness through Planetary Exploration

With little, we've always had
What we needed
So what might a people
Broken down
By the ignorance and fear of weak men
Know intrinsically of a life of zen?

—Wisdom of Colorful Skin

This is it!

Now is all we have

This body and time

Are our access point

To portals and worlds

Within—

And, oh, you think you've seen

A river mighty.

—Awakening

See the world

Open wide

Heart

Soul

Big

Stand inside

Eyes so clear

God can't hide

—Come Out, Come Out, Wherever You Are

Be on an omniversal mission
Because we are limitless
Move in your couch,
Your loveseat,
Your favorite chair,
Your teacups,
Towels, blankets, bed, shoes, clothes
Anything that will fit in there

And buckle in like it's a spaceship
On a voyage through boundless skies
Off into the great beyond
Chasing moonbeams like they're fireflies.
Taking meteor showers
Watching galaxies flower
Walking toward the starlit stair
Mind-moondancin' on spaceships
Floating, ever-woke, aware

—Moondancin' on Spaceships

We rose to shores that felt like sinking sands
Harvested seeds from brittle, barren land
We had no words when they said take a stand
Our voices lost, hoarse, sore, place no demands

We scatter seeds in fields that can't be seen
Because we know with daily watering
Will come a flower rich, winter to spring
Collective mind's eye—creates everything

Our actions kept us steady on the grind
We could have spoken, but that would have taken too much time

We're ever forward—shaping a new Earth
Our moments numbered—each breath equals worth.

They had 'em tied up—all watching the news
They had 'em givin' up—all their rights to choose
They had 'em, and THEY didn't even know
The wheel of life breeds life—an onward flow

Collective mind's eye must be center stage
To halt a juggernaut of multi-century's rage

Collective mind's eye, man against machine?
Collective mind's eye—
Creates Everything.

—Collective Mind's Eye

JOURNEYS
& DREAMS

The realm of universal consciousness can be considered an invisible realm. Initially, it can be seen only by using your mind's eye. The physical world we see every day is the visible realm that we consider to be the "real world." We see it with the same two eyes we can see in the mirror when we look at ourselves. It seems irrational to think that the physical world is secondary to the realm of thought and pure consciousness, but everything happens first in the invisible realm of thought and pure consciousness. Everything must be seen as a reality first through the mind's eye.

It's not enough to venture within to connect with universal consciousness and collect seeds to bring back to the physical world. Each life has a purpose and a path. Each person contributes something to the physical world that was not there before. Many people may encourage you to follow your dreams. Dreams sound fluffy and soft like a cloudy cotton ball, but dreams are work. Work is not to be feared. It is virtuous and gives life purpose. One of the most beautiful things we can do is to love our work. Even if you are not yet working your dream job, if you wake up every day seeing yourself already living your dream, then your intentions will begin to bring your wishes closer to you.

These poems are wishes for the world and whispers of hope that can help light the way on your journey. They are meant to inspire you to awaken your infinite potential and endless creativity. May all of your adventures lead to using your gifts for the good of all living beings, and may all of your wishes come true.

All of life is a celebration
Treating others kindly
Creating true elation
Plant that never bloomed
Now holds a flower
Welcome beauty in
Love every hour

Every thought aligns
With good intentions
All are seen as self
A vast extension
Deed been done to one
To all will blossom
Open, endless well
For all to draw from

Every life is lived
By conscious patterns
Karma has been charged
With heartfelt actions
Presence gifts itself
Adventure, waiting
Wheels of life
Like breath
Fireflies Creating.

—Wishes

All is but a dream.
Dreams are everything.

Every hard time
I've ever had

I dreamed my way out of it.

—Hope / Dream Is the Only Reality

Tapered Purple Aventurine
Ever flowing never seen
Iridescent reflection
Like settled snow
That as soon as witnessed
Saw it go

Cloudscapes cover cobalt seas
Undiscovered pathways freeze
Only one footstep when set here
Can move mountains
Pathways clear
Tapered Purple Aventurine—
Is what it means to have a dream.

—Tapered Purple Aventurine

You have a contract
To live up to who you said
You would be

A star-made contract
To shape the world
As you'd wish to see

Highest potential
Blueprint of your soul

Now is the time
To work and watch
Earth turn to gold

—Star-Made Agreement

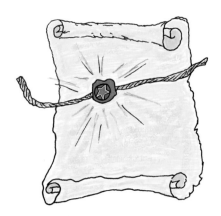

By the time you get to where you are going
Everything you did will seem so small
You will realize that it has always just been
A series of tiny steps.

—Tiny Steps

I wake up
And face my work
Which is always larger than me
Then I remember that my job
Is mostly in the doing
And rarely in the outcome

It is through the doing that
I can afford to trust each step
Ever moving
Toward my dream.

—How to Climb a Mountain

The wall was high
But I knew every stone
For I had built it
On my own
With guided hands
Cracked, splintered, peeled
With back and shoulders—
Like hammers—wield
With shaky bones
Sweaty palms chilled

And every motion—every move
A circle, cycle—joist to groove
Weighted down—each brick to brick
Layered long—make each row fit
Like I had built it once before
And like each time I noticed more

And why guided hands but built alone?

To have ingrained each undertone
Once a blueprint of the soul
Now a fingerprint, embedded code

The wall was high
But I knew every stone
For I had built it
And it made me strong

I had climbed it
And tumbled down
Grazed the surface
Felt endless ground
To see it crumble
The dust of stars
And I am body-less
No cage, no bars

Levitating between grains of sand
Scattered—
Thrown into the air
By guided hands

The wall was high
And I knew every stone
For I had built it
Now, it's gone

—Every Stone

Worthy

Good enough

We will never be

Good enough

Parents

Grandparents

Friends

Family

Lovers

Colleagues

Strangers

Good enough

We will never be good enough

Until

We're gone.

—If the Self Can't See

Anyone

Can do

Anything.

Set your expectations there.

All greatness is needed.

See Beyond.

—Rules

You were always presented

Royally

Although you never thought

Yourself so.

Even if the world were to tell you

Constantly

Being beautiful

Is something *YOU* must know.

—You Must Believe

Seed today

Flower tomorrow

—Believe

I leave to you my dreams

In their tattered skin

With their broken ends

On their crooked roads

Take these shoes

With holes —

Have them shined, resoled

—Re-Souled

Start the day
Tuning yourself
To the light
You came to see
In this world.

—The Mind Is an Age-Old Instrument

There are those who receive blessings
With great ease and little visible labor.

There are those who spend lifetimes
Working toward the glory that is
Reflected many cycles after the first
Seed has been sown.

There are those whose consciousness
Allows them to openly receive a gift
From elders who have done the mundane.

It is always a calling forth of
All directions, of every corner,
Of all fibers of existence.

It is always an alignment of the
Beyond, with the bygone, to the before

Near the between,
Just to believe.

It is always an openness.
An allowance—
An acceptance
Like a light switch.

And a day that seemed long
And a year—after a year
And a life—or two or twelve or twenty—
Any measurement of time

Is equivalent to one and the same.
As your eye begins to awaken
With any measurement of time it has taken
To what has always been there in the making
For you.
For only you.

—Light Switch

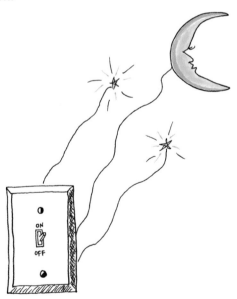

You have turned
Old gray stones to gold
Shaped your thoughts
Into forms to hold
When it rains
Open arms raised high
Catching dream-drops
Like water falling from the sky

Splish and splash
Down the stream of life
Zip and zoom
Ultraviolet light
Made a dance floor
Of the curved full moon
Dust of asteroids
Floating like hot-air balloons

From what you've learned
Salted seas will part
Be found smiling
With whole broken hearts

Sculptors, shape
Shifting points of view
Painters, color
Theories proven true
Builders, craft
Making wishes real
Teachers, lesson
Plan to help all heal

Now found smiling
Whether storms or sun
Been seen soaring
Though life weighs a ton
Out there glowing
On a new moon night

Lucid body
Filled with golden light.

—Seen Golden Lights

What are the chances really?
What are the possibilities?
What is the likelihood
All would fall as it should
And as it fell
That it would be for the greatest good?

—Probability of Positivity

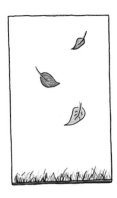

Oh, to be the first leaf
To weave, to spin, to fall
The courage of the first leaf
So powerful and small
Kiss the earth, become the dirt, a blade of grass
Or a tree so tall
Then to understand the first leaf
On your branch
As it shakes
Then spins—

Moves with the wind
To begin again
To trust,
Following nature's call

—The First Leaf

I let the poem move me
It broke my heart, I cried
Somewhere, I probably, even just a little, died

I let the poem sweep me
It gave me a new name
Some word I could not quite pronounce
(I felt a touch of shame)

I let the poem shake me
Like jelly rollin' thighs
That always wanted to be smooth,
Brown, honey to the eyes

I found the poem inside me
It had been all along
Still I had the slightest fear
I'd wake and it'd be gone

—Done as a Poem Will Do

None of us know
What the hell we are doing
How the hell we got here
Why, where, or when we are going
But we know
We are going

Follow a breath
Like a breeze, ever flowing
Enter a land
For a moment, all knowing
There is a place
Always been
Never left
Ever glowing

It is the here-now space
Out of time, Heart base
Snow White, Queen Anne's
Laced with all and none
An endless run
To touch the sun
Remembering
Where
We have come from

—Remember

I love my problems
Because they are mine
And I've got problems
Of the blue to black kind

Take my problems
Count 'em one by one
Blessings
Multiply 'em
By ten thousand life
Lessons

Don't tell me your troubles
I've got enough of my own
These are the words
From an old country song

When I lay dying
And my eyes
Heavy close
Hope I've lived my life
For the highs
And the lows

—The Highs and the Lows

My work
Is a life's work
There have been celebrations
For achievements
But nothing
Like looking back at
My life's work.

Somewhere
There is a book of lives
It holds every life that I have lived
Some lives I lived for fortune
Some lives I lived for fame
Some I lived for love
Some I lived in vain

This life I had a vision
Hoped it would happen fast
But as days mounted years
I worked as moments passed

Sometimes
So unrewarded
A barren, dreamscaped land
Then I'd be led to water—a feast,
Forgetting
Sand-crackled feet—the famine,
And blistered, aching hands

Afraid to rest, so falling into bed
To trust the dream—a test
Two steps back, one step ahead

I worked and waited
For something grand
But it never came—
A bead of sweat—my accolade
My work speaking for my name

The winter of my journey's here,
Collectively I see
The treasure
Of a life's work
Like the rings of an old-growth tree.

—A Life's Work

I was

I came

I went

I loved

I lived

I lent

I gave

I took

I spent

Look back

What has it meant?

—A Life of Meaning

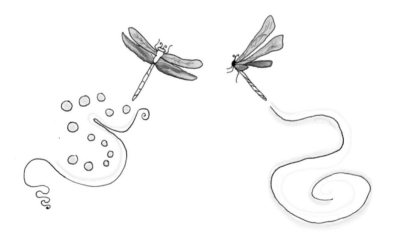

Oh, what would a fairy do
If a fairy could do
What a fairy would do

And who would a fairy be
If a fairy could be
All a fairy could see

And what would a fairy tale
If a fairy could tell what a fairy
Knew well

Only a fairy would know
That the magic starts where your thoughts first flow
And only a fairy could tell
That your heart is an endless wishing well
These are things that a fairy can show
But it's up to you to slip on
Each flying shoe
And to do
What a fairy would do.

—A Fairy Tale

You only have one day

'Til the moon rise sun set down

Only one day

Before the sun rise moon set round

What will you do

And where will you be found

Who will you be

Leave the earth wrapped, love, spellbound

You only have one hour

Before the star shine midnight blue

Just a single hour

'Til the clear sky morning dew

How will you face

This bright day path way new

What words to write

On this blank page lying beneath you

What will be said

Of your star gaze light ship eyes

What could be heard

Of your bird flight 'cross blue skies

Who could have seen

Your moon glow night dance twirls

Who would have guessed

You'd sketch a rainbow-painted world

—Blank Page

When you don't see a path

Before you,

Maybe it's time to fly.

—Visualization

LAMENTATIONS
& TRANSFORMATIONS

It takes such incredible courage to face the impermanence of all forms. After losing a loved one, we can try to avoid the sadness of their transition, but it will eventually surface. Sadness does not have to lead to misery and despair. Loss is a transformation, not only for the person who leaves but also for everyone left behind.

It is a miraculous thing to be in a body and to share the physical world with those we love dearly. Just think of the events that have lined up in precisely the perfect way to bring any two people together in time. Being able to hear a loved one laugh, to see their eyes light up, to reach out and touch them, these are all experiences that can happen only on this physical plane while we are alive.

Nothing of love is ever lost, but all forms do change. Change is our only constant. But those we love may stay with us, may spiritually communicate with us through serendipitous signs like the colors of the setting sun, a butterfly soaring through the air, a street name, or their favorite song coming on the radio. They may also assist us in our own transcendence. Knowing that we too will one day pass, there are things we can do to make sure those we will leave behind know how much we appreciate having this time together. There are things we can say or point out that can be a code for our loved ones to realize our presence when we are no longer in the form of a body. All that we love can leave messages for us written on the sky and in the seasons.

Impermanence reveals itself in every breath. Grief can be a teacher that breaks our hearts open with immeasurable gratitude for each chapter in the book of this lifetime. Though we feel like we have plenty of time and a clock's hands can seem to tick-tock by ever so slowly, a single life lasts no longer than the sighting of a shooting star. These are poems to help us wade through the waters of sorrow when they arise.

You must walk
Through the front door.
With grief there is no other way
With most things there are other avenues, many paths
That lead to the same place
But with grief, you must
Go to the driveway
Step onto the porch
Reach out your hand to knock
Only to find
It is already open
As if it was waiting
For you
Only you
To enter through the front door.

There is a spirit self gained
And a worldly self left behind
And where you thought you had a choice
You are surely soon to find—

You must walk
Through the front door.

—A Light Beyond

There is a space.
It has always been there.
For you.
For
You.
I tried friends, I tried poems,
I tried songs,
But none belong.
There is a space
For you.

Where the lens was blurry
Where the winds don't hurry
And though the world won't cease to turn
It has been such a heart-aching thing to learn
It has been with salted, wilted tears that burn
That there is a space for you.
Can't be hidden—like all things true.
It's only a body, and the spirit flew
But here in me . . .
There will always be
A space for you.

—For You

Forty-one years.
What do I know? Outside looking in
At twenty up 'til thirty-three—
Looked pretty rough to me.
But they pushed on through
And the time, how it flew
He was working, got sick
She was raising, they had six
Empty nesting, counting blessings
On to master life's toughest lesson.
As they lowered him down—
Friends and family stood 'round
Meals were served, condolences heard
A once-busy house holds now not a word
She sits looking at time
Things were rough, things were fine
A love that never knew rings
A love bound only by heartstrings
It knew little success
Was constantly put to the test
But the heart's strings are so strong
That they can reach out so long
And even though he has gone
She knows she's not alone.

—Forty-One Years

Thirty-four years.
It's now I see
Inside looking out at forty-one
It's in the staying
That true beauty is known.

—Thirty-Four Years

Sick was on my tongue
But I got up there anyway

Wickedness

Had my thoughts off their track

Fired by chains
Broken by strings
That were steel tied

Steel Tied

How can hearts that are steel tied
Ever even hope to happily abide?

How can chains that are broken by strings
Feel free when they steel bind me?

Oh to fly—
Oh to soar—
Oh to, Oh two
Oh two people turn three, four
Oh two, Oh to
Oh today he was here
Oh tomorrow he'll be gone
Oh two—Oh too
Much for me to bear
He is gone
But he's still there
Oh two—
We are
Steel Tied.

—Steel Tied

You broke my heart the day you said hello
'Cause all that's sure to come
Is sure to go
I will not be a beggar by the fire
Because I know that truth is just a liar
Perspective is the only truth that's real
You bend it, shape it, mold it with your will
I will not be a pauper, peach, or pear
Because I know true love is ever there
For it is in the cracks, the breaks, the seams
And it is in the spaces in between
It is in the shadows
Fragments, grain
It is in the dust from which you came
You broke my heart the day you said hello
'Cause all that's sure to come
Is sure to go
Go back toward the place it first began
To rise and shine
New form, but never end

—Of Heartbreak

I love you
Like a fall leaf dancing
And twirling in the wind
Softly landing,
Returning to the warm earth
Rest
Make new
Begin
Again

—Comfortably

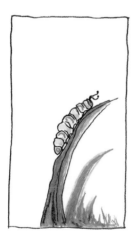

Though the waves of life may rise
When they fall, there lies a prize
Nothing living ever dies.

Life is endless, death is too
But don't let this baffle you
Out of time, each moment new
Must breathe deep
To know this truth.

Here is there and back again
This is how it's always been
Where you end, there you begin
Through the stillness,
Be the wind.

Nothing living ever dies
This might come as a surprise
Look around, you'll see it's clear
Changing form of all things dear.

—Nothing Living Ever Dies

It is okay to grieve an old dream.

You cross the emotional sea
And those hopes become memories
That you still keep as sacred
That you store behind glass.

Reaching shores of a new dream
Can take such bravery
But then it seems that you've
Never had any other hope.
The landscape is beautifully suited
With adornments fitting for your
Present state.
There are no doubts that
You have made the right choices
That you have been guided in the right directions
That you are in the perfect place
Where you were always
Meant to be.
It is a dance.
It is yours.
No other can ever be in that space.

—To Grieve an Old Dream

I want to die saying thank you

To everything flashing before my eyes as I slip away

Thank

You

They say you see your entire life

In what seems like a blink.

Guess I've got some ever-present work to do.

Filling my cup with things I want to drink.

—Creating a Life of Magical Moments

```
I am all
And All is me
We are all
We'll always be
Death is all in life that's free
It is not a mystery
The All in All
Is all that's key
```

—All

Godspeed travels in light waves

In spite of how mankind behaves

Cause Godspeed moves in its own time

Faster than a bullet

Pace beyond mind

Godspeed graces all that will be was

Godspeed zooms by just because

Felt it

Did it happen

Couldn't tell ya what it was

Godspeed doing just the thing it always does

Godspeed took my friend and left me blue

That is just a simple thing Godspeed will do

Out of body

Out of mind

Godspeed is true

To a cause that's bigger than me, omniversal view.

—Interstellar

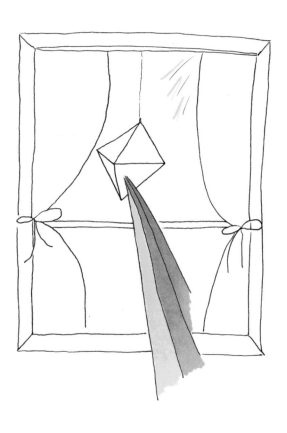

You'll lose the ones

You were never gonna keep

Playin'

You'll move the ones

You'd never thought you'd reach

Just sayin'

And raise the arms

Of hearts that wildly beat—hands

Swayin'

Then leave the world

Heavy tongue-tied tickled pink

But who's weighin'?

—Fearlessly Forward

I do not cry for the dying
But for the living
The living they'd yet to do
The living they'd yet to see
The yearnings they'll never know
The longings, dreams, hopes, beliefs

A walk down a road now paved
Sunrise of a brand-new day
To witness a lover age
Life's book—turn another page

To fight and to make amends
More time shared with loving friends
To watch something new begin
Rewrite how a story ends

I will not cry for the dying
But it is sad to see them go
Hiccups of black salt wilted tears
Is all the sorrow that I can show.

—For the Living

EARTH &
OTHER WORLDS

Earth is a magical realm. If we can transcend and live in the invisible world of endless potential, then the earth becomes our playground. It can be a canvas. It can be as malleable as clay.

Through exploring the magic of Earth, other enchanting worlds begin to reveal themselves. These worlds blossom within our physical world and eventually go beyond. We start to see that a glass of water is not just a glass of water. It is the hands of the person who made the glass. It is the rivers and oceans. It is the elements that were here long before human beings existed. Drinking a glass of water can begin to feel like you are tasting the stars with a twist of a few galaxies on the side. It can be a potion with the power to change life as we know it.

Mother Earth is continuously trying to communicate with us. The environment is in a state of emergency. We are facing a climate crisis. But miraculous things can happen when we are living mindfully. The smallest steps to respect the earth could positively shift the planet faster than we could ever dream would be possible. Each citizen of Earth has this power each day. The elixir of stardust is everywhere. Everything holds an iridescent glow if you are open to seeing it. No matter what direction you set out toward in the world, there is always light around you. There is light in even the darkest moments of your life. It's just: Can you see it? Are you aware, and are you willing to let the light guide the way?

I came

To bask in the sun

To see my mother's smile

To dream, to see manifested

But while I'm here and

So thus far invested—

I guess I'll

Roll up my sleeves

And kneel down on my knees

Planting flowers and seeds

So Earth will know—

That I have blessed it.

—Giving Back with Gratitude

Do you know who I am?
We met so long ago.
I've always been
Inside you.

I am thinking
Of how hard
My heart had to get
To leave you.

It was hard
But you treated it
Delicately
Like an eggshell
In your hands.

—To Find Yourself

Did you get to see the last frost melt
And the spring grass popping through?

Or the moon set, sun rise, down
With the fall leaves drinking dew?

Or the clovers bunching up
Forming patches—did you play?

Growing back year after year
Find a four-leafed one
Someday?

—How Was Your Trip to Earth This Time?

This world

Look up

Glued eyes

Open wide

There is a world!

And you are missing me.

—iWorld (Exist)

I took the world

And looked at it upside down

Was quite surprising

All the love I found

An Escher drawing

Entered secret doors

I had to ask myself

Was that there before?

And sure enough it had been all along

But life was busy

Had my eyes glued to my phone.

—iWorld (Exist) II

And how about an appreciation for it all

The picture hanging on the wall

The dust that settled

Though you were too busy

To watch it fall

Books you wish to read

Places you'll save to go

Faces you hope to see

Who you are

And who you wish to be

How and when

Where and why

What and who

And oh so many things

Left on earth to do . . .

—After Physical Formation / Material Body

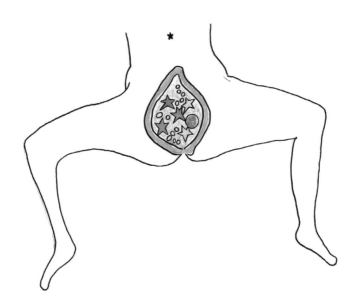

Just as we
Find ourselves
Living some place
We find ourselves

On Earth

Can we ever really remember
The reason we stay where we are?
And doesn't the reason we are where we are
Change as we are where we are?

And aren't we now
Planning to be where we will be soon?
And will we remember nine years into
Where we would have been soon
What we had planned
And why we had chosen the plan
We'd planned at that moment?
Sometimes I (we) cannot remember what I did yesterday
But I have a pretty good idea of what I'd like to do tomorrow

So when we wonder how we got to the place we are,
How we got to Earth,
Would it not be the same?

—Can Anyone Remember How We Got Here?

They are all so beautiful

I am so happy we have found each other

We are all rich in Self

We found ourselves within the world that Is

We stopped

Asking the world to be what it is not and

Started to appreciate what it has always been

It cradled us

It sheltered us

It ever-so-generously

Gave and gave quantumly-quantum leap

To unfold—for all who seek

Woven, winding, enter, twined

Twisted, tossed, yours is mine

Look inside, gold to find

Check again, dust of time

Echoes, spin, air to sing

Buzz of bees

Hums all things

Om and om

Ah and ah

Oh-e-oh

All things glow

Om-e-om

All in all

Speckled spackled

Quilt to sew

—Quilt of Life

Be enchanted by the little worlds

A plant

A wall

A door . . .

A shadow cast

Because it means

There's light

To help you soar.

—Little Worlds

The Blues
Was
The other world.

It was a place of freedom.

History can make you a prisoner.
What world do you wish to see?
Live there.
Learn what you can of the past,
But don't let it keep you from living free.
Of the other world
Live there.

Refuse to accept any binding chains of the present.
Of the other world
Live there.

—Slave Mind Blues

Ode to Fuckin' Feelin':
And where shall we go from here?!
I don't wanna be a Folk Star, Blues Star, Pop Star . . .
I just wanna BE n feel n be felt . . .
And Oh to FUCKING FEEL!!!
And can this world take a black girl
With magic that won't fit its box,
Can it take real and unshapely hair
Flowing in true, thick locs?
Do we in colors still need chains to recognize ourselves,
Or can we see into the future toward what our ancestors
Would have hoped for our modern-day selves?
And by now our ancestors—
Colorless . . .
Blood rich, red thick,
Heartsick, can't forget . . .
So human in all shades that who'd give a shit . . .
And by now our souls united do sing
In harmonies and melodies of human strings

—Ode to Fuckin' Feelin'

My world is filled with charm

I welcome you unarmed

For my world is filled with harmony

I am the softest song

A heart so kind

A sweet-souled gentle mind

But please don't take this lightly

Because

Yes Suh, I am quite aware of the temperature held by these
     times.

Of the maniacs—who bulldoze the innocent

Of the tyrants—some may call leaders

Of the genocides—of the darkest corners

Where our greatest demons hide . . .

But it is mine to decide.

It is mine to make right

And I'm gon' tell ya baby

I ain't comin' here to fight

So when you enter my door,

Put down your blades

Leave your devils at the gate

No cell phones, no TVs, no radios

No eggshells, no tightropes, no tiptoes

Come in here and sit with me.

Let's be the change we wish to see.

It's not to talk
It is to do
It is to know an inner truth
It is a power we all hold
But we will so easily
Let it be bought
Let it be sold.
It is a power that once revealed
Can shift a planet and make change real.

—Make Change Real

A vote can be just a check mark on a page
I'd rather see a thirsty heart rattlin' a cage
Give me water
Or feel and hear my rage
We are living in a blind, rich age

At our hands all problems could be saved
But once a ballot's cast, we've done our part
Just wipe our hands, it's not our issue,
The path's been paved
Elected official, but he's just a mask for a path we have made
Let's take our power
Now is the hour
For each heart to awaken
And in kindness flower

So who holds the pen?
Is it women, or is it men?
Or is it you,
Yes, meaning you
In the shoes you're standing in?
Tell me who . . . with every motion
All in action
Without the news as a distraction
Holds the pen?

—Responsibilities after Voting

Who are we?

To be creative?

To try to change the world without becoming politicians

To try to give people inspiration

To be—

Be simply great and absolutely wonderful

To create worlds

Within this world

Yeah, to just

And just

Just who the hell

Are

WE?

—Who Are We?

In the same way
That you shy away
From hearing about
The blood that gushes
From my body
Every month

May you shy
Away from
Making laws
That tie my
Uterus in chains
And turn my stomach
To a lump

Sir, should I wear a pad
Or a tampon today?
Or should I just bleed
Where I stand
As I break under
Your command?

Life is precious
This is true

So let us end all wars
That's a mother's living son—
Let us have affordable health care
That's a father's living daughter—
Let us take back our grocery store shelves
That's a few rounds of chemo we might be able to save—
Elect leaders who'll support laws
To reduce our carbon footprint,
Keep a closer eye
On how our government's dollars
Are being spent,
Plant gardens in the ghettos,
Stop gunning down the negroes,
Stop living for fake Trump gold,
Start kindness, practice, heal souls.

Life is precious
This is true

Let us create a more harmonious
Earth to welcome
Babes brown, white, red, black, or blue!

—The Living

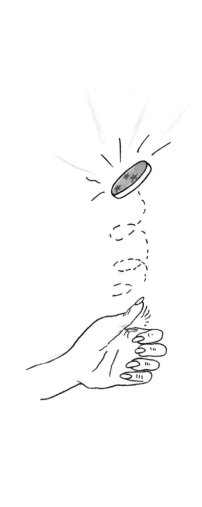

People just want

Their shoes kicked off

With their toes curled up

And their hair let down

And their frown turned 'round

With their loved ones near

Dog-cussed

Still held dear

With their dollas rollin'

Three times plus the bills they owin'

Give a bangin' deal

On an overpriced Amazon return—damn near steal

Give a trip or two

To a lake nearby

Or to the local zoo

Ain't got to be much

Just want something new

People just want a life that's true

Ain't gotta cost much

But a change will do

Living in a time of high crime

From the wealthiest office

To the welfare line

Yes, a change will do

How did it get ever so complicated

But there it is

The way we've made it

—A Change Will Do

In everything I saw,

It seemed,

I'd seen a touch before.

As if upon acknowledgment,

Then I would see a door

As if when viewed with full belief

I'd walk through and see more

As if a blade of grass could hold the answers I sought for

A single river wave

Would bring a goddess to my shore

A raindrop on a windowsill

Could be a portal to explore

The color blue, if seen at night

Should shake my worries down to the floor

A politician's words would spread like butter on a sword

And all opinions fade

As spirit moves up ever forward

I hold the pen, but all that's written flows,

Like done before

From songs unsung

I'd sing,

A voice a crackle to the ears

I'd sing a song bright as the sun

With notes so sharp they'd pierce

An unforgettable sound, so strange, so awkward,

Strong and fierce

I'd sing a song it seemed I'd sung—
I'd sung it once before.
I'd sing a song it seemed I'd sung—
A bodhisattva's song to sing
A song to sing and sing and sing—
We sing it once, twice, in between
We sing.
We sing.
We sing.

—Bodhisattva's Song to Sing

Earthlings,

I'm not giving up on you.

—The Goddess

They call me strange
'Cause I see gods and goddesses at every turn
Be it a tree, person, butterfly, river,
Mountain, concrete, or sea
They are all gods and goddesses to me.

—Gods and Goddesses

Now that I am gone

I cannot believe

How many days of my life

I missed watching the sunset

—When I Was on Earth

Inside the mirrored space I stood
Without a question of bad or good
No judge to sentence
Just myself
Another life, just after death?
Or should I rest and meditate
In starlit spaces radiate
Perhaps for seconds to centuries wake
No need to hurry, I won't be late
For here and now, time has no weight
Though thoughts are flowing
They take no shape

I can remember all events from form
I can remember being—born
I am reflecting on actions made
On every role that I had played

There are the choices some would call good
But for another, didn't work as they should
There are decisions I made out of fear
Then take a note, upon return to make clear

Multiples of repetitions, but still the same sum
Subtractions and additions, divided still equaling one
And I could stay here forever, but I know I must return
Choose some parents, get a body
And practice what I've learned.

—To Return / Between Death and Rebirth

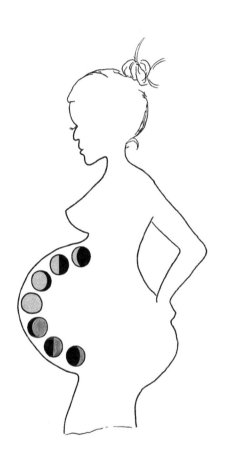

MINDFULNESS, MANTRAS & MEDITATIONS

How can we keep our minds steady?

It is not easy to live a life of calm and peace. Unfortunately, not everyone can live in a monastery. The mind can be a creature of its own volition, but we don't have to follow it down every one of its wandering paths. Luckily, we can choose which path to follow. So how can we live mindfully in the modern world? No set way will work for every person, but there are gentle practices to train our minds to be aware of who is making the calls.

These poems are reminders of the importance of being your own guru.

Find your stillness.

Live life in total awareness.

Keep a mantra that works for you on constant repeat in your mind so that you can call on it, especially when your battery is running low.

Surrender with each breath, and be ready to welcome the greatest gifts life has to offer you. Learn your life's rhythm. Know when to go and when to press pause, to sit alone for clarity and to visualize the world you wish to see. Realize this is a life's work. Have patience and find joy—all things are your teachers. Everything is a guide. Enjoy being. Appreciate where you are. Know that you are already where you wish to be in the invisible realm. Believe that you can make all things focused, practiced, and seen in the invisible world come to pass in the visible world--or at least why not die trying?

Be strong and soft. Follow your soul.
Live in gratitude for all that is.

Realize-remember-recognize that you are the oneness of all.
An insect on the window—that is you!
The trunk of a tree,
The wings of a bumblebee,
They are you too!
You will fail, and you will fall.
Sometimes you'll have to beg and sometimes be so weary
That you will even crawl.
But the light,
The light is always there
If you keep steady with your practice and live your life
Aware.
Bask in it.

What is your favorite mantra?

Can you repeat it all day?

As you make the bed,

As you drink tea,

You head to work,

On and off the subway,

When you read a book,

When you hear a song,

When you're in a crowd,

Or if you feel alone.

Can you keep your mantra steady?

It could be while just following each breath,

Or it could be as you are walking,

Or when you sit to meditate.

Find your path

From birth until death.

Where is your mind? Can you keep it focused on your path?

—Mindfulness

Blue moon sprinkle duster
Star face sparkle truster
Black night firelight
Candle stacked balloon rustler
Hand-drawn silk wearing
Felt-haired sun shiner
Windblown answer seeking
Hard rain heart a-beating
Dance fast foot tapping
Sit still mind poet rapping
Sit still mind poet
Sit still mind
Sit still
Sit
Sit still
Still
Still

—Magic of Mindset

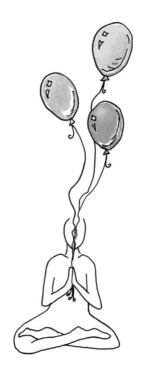

Be who you'd be in the room
If everything were as perfect
As you'd envisioned it would be.
Be the greatest.

—Born to Be

One of the best prayers
That I have ever prayed:

Thank you for everything
You have done

I trust you.

—Surprise Me!

Thank you, goddess, for this life
Thank you, goddess, for this time

Root to leaf and leaf to vine
Circle, cycle, dot to line

All things shimmer, all things glow
Small is large, to those who know

Them that know can never tell
Each must walk toward the well

Though we journey side by side
Them that know might even guide

But for you, can't make a move
Only guide you—yours to choose

And they'll never share your face
Only guide you to the place

And they'll never wear your shoe
Each footprint's different
So each pathway's new

Thank you, goddess, for this life
Thank you, goddess, for this time

Root to leaf and leaf to vine
Circle, cycle, dot to line

—A Goddess Mantra (To Be Repeated)

Wake and feel
The restlessness with no name
Itch and toss
Tingle, burn
Long, sit, silent, learn.

Find a sacred space in the day
And stay.

Rinse, wash, repeat.

—Cure for the Restlessness with No Name

I am meant to wander
I am meant to roam
I am meant to see the world
But never leave my home.

Gently turn
My gaze low
Sit with legs crossed
Breathe slow
Colors soften
Starlight
Awakening
The true sight
Twinkle, sparkle
Take flight
Effervescent
Luminescent
Iridescent
Satellite

—The Mind's Eye

Delight in the exuberance of life
Demand excellence in all you do
Pay attention to the things you do
And the reasons you do them.
Walk proudly down the street
Pay attention to the way you hold your head
—The way your eyes gaze
Across the moments of your life.

Look for smiles on others' faces
If you do not see a smile anyplace
Look for smiles in others' souls
Extract complete and total happiness
From each moment of life
Although some times may be bittersweet
Savor the bitterness like a lemon in
Cool water on the hottest southern summer day.

This is your time.
You have come.

Give thanks for each and every being that has
Come to teach and celebrate at your side
Pay attention to where you sit in a room
The way you dress your body
Chew your food
Breathe in air
Each moment is a different breath
You will never breathe the same air twice
Sitting in the same chair
Eating the same fruit
Biting from the same exact curve of its succulent skin
With the same thought on your mind.

This is your time.

Enjoy this life.
Learn its lessons.
You will never come this way
In this same body
Again.

—Sacredness of All Things

Sip tea—like there is no place to be

Drink wine—like you've got plenty of time

Make wishes—like you can move mountains

Let dreams flow—like they're from water fountains

Catch falling leaves

Count blessings in threes

Ask guidance from trees

Spread hopes on the wind like they're wildflower seeds

And when you are asked

What you believe

Speak the truth—that what you give is what you receive

—Being (Oh to Live!)

God says,

"What more do you need?"

You say,

"Well, I never lived in my dream home

It wouldn't have to be big

It wouldn't have to be a fortune

It could be small

As long as it was cute and clean."

Then God says,

"What have you done with the home I gave you?

You are a creator

Just like me—my image

You told me

'It wouldn't have to be big

It wouldn't have to be a fortune

It could be small'

I left it up to you to make it cute and keep it clean."

—What It's Like to Have Soul

There is light
Around every shadow
Train your eyes
To see them both.

—Perspectives

A strong woman
Can still have a soft heart
A smart woman
Can have a gentle mind
So don't let this world
Tell you who you've gotta be
To let your brightest light shine
Gonna have some hard lessons
Turn them into sweet blessings
Lily-scented, butter-softened belly gold
Keep a laugh ever ready
Hold a thought-mantra steady
Repetition for when the world feels cold
A wise woman
Knows the paths are many
Close her eyes, take old back roads
While others are busy drawing maps
She trusts the guide that whispers
Follow your soul

—Tincture and Tonic

Put on your cloak of pure perfection
And head raised walk out the door
Don't let the weight of your imperfections
Keep your chin lowered toward the floor
It's in the push, the strive, the shovel, drive,
The twist, toss, pull, the turn,
That you'll begin to slowly rise
Like smoke as a wild flame burns
Every day a phoenix new
From the ash
Sparkle
Blemished jewel
Gather faults, failures, losses, pain
To be used as alchemic fuel
Perfectly imperfect
As you are
Show up each day without fear
To live flawlessly is like trying to extract
The salt from a single tear

—Perfectly Imperfect

Failure is not a loss unless you settle for it.

Buddha was a beggar
For his alms, but not on his knees
And he taught the simplest truth
1-2-3 to A-B-Cs

God is busy painting
Polka dots on the leaves
Always asking us to join
In the colorful festivities

See a rainbow
Lucky
Watch a moon phase
Charmed
Catch the sunset
Fortunate
Hug the planet
With both arms

Living life connecting
With the beauty of it all
Finding joy throughout life's seasons
Summer, Winter, Spring, or Fall

—Joy in Each Moment

All that was and All that is
Got together to form a cause
That would change what had not yet been
Story rewritten, from beginning 'til end

Frozen moments where all exist
Would be defrosted with a light, cool mist
Chosen careful—from a bird's-eye view
To create something golden, iridescent hue

Wand to wield and given free will
Forming worlds—intention, thought, act, feel
Conscious creations, planetary explorations
Earth elevation, a uniting of all nations

What could never be and what we hoped to see
All woven together like a tapestry
With a stitch in time, we could save more than nine
Changing course—set a mindful trajectory

—Dust of Stars

Touch five tree trunks
As you make your way to work.
This is a healing for worry
And protection for your heart
Medicine for the spirit's soul
And the best way
For the day to start.

—Spirit's Spell

Every time

You step out

The door

Be ready

To be

Of service.

—Giving

To my family, thank you for dreaming such beautiful dreams and sharing your journeys with me. We are a family of dreamers. You give me the courage to believe that anything is possible. Let's keep painting iridescent rainbows around the moon.

To my friends, thank you for inspiring me by being incredible humans who keep me uplifted. I love exploring the world with you and hope you understand that I've kept these years of writing poems and making drawings a little secret between me and the fairies.

To Amanda Lucidon, thank you for changing my life with one question. "What are you working on that you are madly in love with?" My answer was that I was writing every day since my father passed away. You then waved your magic wand and connected me to Rachel Vogel, your literary agent. The rest is stardust and golden. May we always be lucky enough to be madly in love with the work we are doing.

To the Grounded Team, thank you for inviting me to join you as we chase the light in every moment. We are light workers. We're only at the beginning of sharing our visions that use art to change the world.

To Rachel Vogel, thank you for believing in my poetry from the moment we shared our first cup of tea.

To Allison Adler and everyone at Andrews McMeel, thank you for believing in poetry and giving so many incredible poets a publishing home to share our words and artwork.

To Matthew, thank you for coming home to a house covered in sketchbooks, crayons, colored pencils, paint, and poems, with a few musical instruments on the side. You are my morning, my evening, my night and Noon. (Nope, it's not a typo. I call him Noon!)

To my readers, may these poems serve as little maps that help guide you continuously back to your inner light, your center, and your compass. You hold keys to such immeasurable beauty, so remember to venture bravely and courageously within, where life's greatest treasures await you!

About the Author

Valerie June Hockett is a singer, songwriter, and
multi-instrumentalist from Tennessee. She's been
hailed by the *New York Times* as one of America's "most
intriguing, fully formed new talents." She has recorded
two critically acclaimed bestselling solo albums and
has also written songs for legendary artists, such as
Mavis Staples and the Blind Boys of Alabama. When she's
not touring, she splits her time between Tennessee and
New York. This is her first book.